Original title:
Frozen Dreams and Winter Gleams

Copyright © 2024 Creative Arts Management OÜ
All rights reserved.

Author: Lucas Harrington
ISBN HARDBACK: 978-9916-94-564-3
ISBN PAPERBACK: 978-9916-94-565-0

The Lightness of a Snowy Dawn

A snowflake landed on my nose,
I sneezed and watched it dance and doze.
With giggles echoing through the trees,
I swore I heard the snowmen tease.

The sun peeked out, it gave a wink,
And ice cubes floated in my drink.
Oh, what a joy, the world so bright,
As squirrels attempted a snowball fight.

Chasing shadows in a winter haze,
With penguin waddles and silly ways.
My mittens stuck, or was it me?
A slippery slope to pure glee!

Snow angels laugh, it's pure delight,
As they tumble, no fear of height.
And when they fall, oh what a sight,
Winter's pranksters, a frosty night.

Frosty Textures of a Sleeping World

A scarf tied tight, I look like a bum,
Tripping over snow, I feel so dumb.
The trees wear coats of bright white fluff,
While fuzzy mittens just aren't enough.

In the distance, a snowman's hat,
I swear it's starting to chat and spat.
'Bring me a carrot!' he cries so loud,
While bouncing children leap, so proud.

Car tires spin, like they're in a dance,
While dogs leap high, giving it a chance.
Chasing tails in circles, what a spree,
With icicles hanging off the marquee.

Oh, winter wind, you tease just so,
With gusty giggles, off we go.
Through snowball fights and frosty dives,
I can't help but love these silly lives!

Dreaming in a Wonderland of White

Snowflakes drifting down with glee,
I think they're throwing a snowball spree.
Sledding with penguins all in a line,
But they just want to steal my hot chocolate sign.

Snowmen gossip in a chilly crowd,
Claiming snowflakes dance—oh, so proud!
But one just slipped and went for a dive,
Now he's rolling, trying to survive!

Glistening Pines in Winter's Dress

Pines wear their coats made of crystal light,
Twinkling like stars, oh, what a sight!
Squirrels on skis zoom up and down,
Wearing little hats, oh, how they frown!

Icicles hang like a disco ball,
While a brave raccoon prepares to stall.
He slips and slides with a comical flair,
Landing right in a snowdrift, unaware!

A Shrouded Glow in the Stillness

Moonlight dances on the frozen ground,
Keeping secrets that might astound.
Mice in scarves throw a winter bash,
While the cat plots for a sneaky clash.

Frosty air filled with giggles and cheer,
As hot cocoa mustaches appear.
Yet a snowball shoots and causes a fuss,
Now everyone ducks, just a little bit fluss!

Secrets Hidden Beneath the Ice

Under the frost lies a hidden show,
Where ice skates dance in a frosty glow.
Fish in formal wear glide to and fro,
Chasing the worm with quite the grand flow!

Secrets are whispered in the chilly breeze,
While ducks on skates learn how to tease.
One takes a tumble, quacking in surprise,
As snowflakes burst into sparkly cries!

Quietude in Winter's Grasp

In the silence, snowflakes dance,
A squirrel slips, lost in a trance.
Hot cocoa spills on winter's chill,
While snowmen plot their magic thrill.

Chill winds howl, they start to tease,
A snowball fight brings laughter's ease.
With frosty bites and giggles bright,
Snowball battles last through the night.

Shimmering Icicles and Muted Hues

Icicles hang like teeth on a grin,
Nature's diamonds, a frozen win.
They shine like chandeliers so grand,
A winter's joke, by nature's hand.

With mittens mismatched, we waddle and slide,
Looking for fun, but oh, what a ride!
Laughs echo while we tumble and fall,
Winter antics, enjoyed by all.

Lullabies of the Falling Snow

Snowflakes whisper, soft and light,
Under moonbeams, a sight so bright.
In pajamas, we dance with glee,
As flurries play hide and seek with me.

Beneath the stars, snowmen conspire,
To steal our hats, their one desire.
With carrot noses and cheeky grins,
They plot a snowball fight, let's begin!

Frost-Kissed Fantasies

Winter winks with a frosty blink,
Trees wear coats, don't you think?
Hot chocolate spills in giggly fits,
As we dodge snowballs, just for kicks.

The ice rink twirls, with laughter we glide,
Falling and laughing, it's one wild ride.
With frosty cheeks and spirits so bright,
Winter's antics bring pure delight.

The Beauty of a Whispering Winter

Flakes dance like little clowns,
While snowmen wear silly frowns.
A gust of wind gives them a shove,
As if they're all in search of love.

Pine trees wear coats, all fluffy and bright,
But squirrels think it's a snack, a bite!
Chasing tails, they trip and slide,
On icy floors, they never hide.

A Symphony of Silence in the Snow

The snowflakes play a soft tune,
While penguins disco under the moon.
They slide on ice with glee and cheer,
Bumping into each other near.

A snowball flies, a comical fight,
As laughter echoes on this white night.
In frozen silence, giggles bloom,
Creating a cozy, joyful room.

Frosted Horizons and Starry Wonders

Stars blink like eyes in a giggly mood,
While rabbits hop in their fuzzy brood.
They nibble on carrots, plotting a prank,
As owls hoot softly from their branchy plank.

Marshmallow clouds float on high,
As snowflakes swirl, oh my oh my!
They tickle noses, make cheeks red,
Winter's fun keeps laughter widespread.

Echoing Stillness of Crystal Dreams

Icicles hang like chandeliers,
While polar bears dance without fears.
They twirl and spin, a goofy sight,
As snowmen cheer with pure delight.

In the stillness, a snowman sneezes,
Sending flakes that tease and tease.
Laughter tumbles like snow downhill,
Creating joy that time can't still.

Whispers in the Icy Breeze

A snowman tried to dance with glee,
But fell down flat, oh what a spree!
With carrot nose in disarray,
He offered up a frosty ballet.

Sleds zoom past, kids scream in cheer,
But one lost mitt, oh dearie me here!
Tumbling down a hill so slick,
Their laughter rings like a magic trick.

Snowflakes Dance in Serenity

Snowflakes pirouette in the night,
Each one a sprite in fluffy white.
They giggle as they float and glide,
Making snowball fights a wild ride.

A penguin slipped on one fine day,
It waddled off in a humorous sway.
The trees all chuckled, branches deep,
As winter's choir sang us to sleep.

The Enchantment of Winter's Caress

A squirrel with acorns, bold and spry,
Is building a nest in the chilly sky.
With nutty plans that make us grin,
He fumbles, slips, and starts again.

Hot cocoa spills across the floor,
As kids run wild and beg for more.
Marshmallows float in a frosted dream,
While parents ponder, or so it seems.

Radiance in the Bitter Cold

Icicles hang like shiny bling,
As penguins gather for a fling.
They waddle, slip, and trip with flair,
Polka-dot hats, a stylish pair.

Timid rabbits hop with glee,
While foxes prance like they are free.
In the ice, a slip leads to grace,
With laughter echoing in this place.

Cosmic Traces in the Wintry Sky

Stars twinkle like ice cubes above,
Wishing they could join the snowball shove.
Galaxies dance in a chilly breeze,
While penguins skate with remarkable ease.

Comets zoom like joy on skates,
Chasing squirrels and slippery mates.
The moon's laughter echoes bright,
As snowmen giggle in sheer delight.

Radiant Reflections on a Frozen Lake

The lake's a mirror, tales untold,
Where fish wear hats, too brave and bold.
They wiggle and splash in shimmering light,
In search of snacks, oh what a sight!

Not quite a boat, just a gliding cat,
Paddling past a snowman's hat.
With every ripple, joy does bloom,
As ducks throw parties, still in costume!

The Enigma of Frost's Caress

Frost bites softly, plays disguise,
Leaving splashes of humor in our eyes.
Each crystal prance, a trickster's plan,
As penguins plot with a cheeky span.

Icicles dangle like toothpicks bright,
While snowflakes giggle, taking flight.
Is it coldness or a playful tease?
Nature's jest, a whimsical breeze!

Dappled Light through Frosty Branches

Branches wear coats of white and gray,
As squirrels perform in a ballet display.
The sun peeks through with a wink and grin,
While snowballs fly, let the fun begin!

Each twinkle sparkles, a chuckle's tune,
As foxes frolic beneath the moon.
Frosted giggles float on the air,
In this silly dance, no one has a care!

Luminous Haze of the Frosted Dawn

Chilly mornings make me frown,
While my coffee tries to drown.
Snowflakes fall, a soft ballet,
I trip on ice while trying to play.

Wacky snowmen stand so tall,
I wonder who made that giant ball?
With carrots poked in, quite absurd,
Their smiles hide secrets, so unheard.

Boots too small, they squeak and slide,
My dog just loves this winter ride.
Chasing snowballs, he makes me laugh,
I'll need new pants, not just a scarf!

The sun peeks out, a cheeky tease,
Chased away by frosty breeze.
Dreams of keeping warm inside,
But here I am, the fun's the ride!

Enigmas of the Winter Veil

Once upon a snowball toss,
I lost my mittens, what a loss!
They vanished in the swirling white,
Did they escape? Outrageous plight!

Footprints zigzag like a dance,
My neighbor's gone, still no sign of chance.
Did he fall or fly away?
The snowman's giggles, led astray!

Sipping cocoa by the fire,
Snowflakes come like a dance choir.
Carols sung by cats outside,
Their yowls and howls a winter tide!

Just when I think it's all in jest,
The plow arrives, I'm off the guest list.
"Thanks for the drifts!" I shout in jest,
Winter's leaving soon, and I need rest!

Drifting in Midnight's Serenity

Stars above in cozy glow,
I stumble through the heaps of snow.
What's that sound? A snore out loud,
Oh look, it's just my dog—so proud!

The moon looks down in a cheeky grin,
While rabbits hop and spin and spin.
I slip on ice, a graceful fall,
Winter nights, oh how they enthrall!

Snowmen gossip, seek some fame,
"Who wore it best?" they play their game.
With carrot noses pointed high,
They're critiquing under this moonlit sky!

Hot chocolate waits, with marshmallows bright,
Time to toast, and laugh tonight!
With every slip and frosty sigh,
Winter's antics make me fly!

Celestial Snowfall and Distant Echoes

Flakes of wonder start to fall,
I gear up for that snowball brawl.
But wait! My mittens are still at home,
A frosty fate, I have to roam!

Frozen fingers twitch and tease,
I scream, "Hot cocoa, please, oh please!"
The squirrels stare, they plot and plan,
To steal my snacks—oh sneaky clan!

Icicles dangle, sharp and bright,
Will they catch my hat in mid-flight?
With every gust, my laughter rings,
Winter mischief makes me sing!

Underneath this starry coat,
I sigh and laugh, a winter boat.
So bring on the chill, the giggles swell,
These joyful frosts? Oh, I can't dwell!

Secrets Encased in Icy Veils

In a world of chilly pranks,
Snowmen dance with goofy ranks.
A penguin slips, a snowball flies,
While winter's giggles fill the skies.

Hot cocoa's warmth and marshmallow cheer,
Frostbitten toes, but who's to fear?
The rabbit wears a scarf too tight,
His hopping style is quite the sight.

Snowflakes swirl with cheeky flair,
Each one lands, a frosty dare.
Sledding down the hill so fast,
We laugh and play, joy unsurpassed.

Icicles hang like shiny swords,
Winter's jesters with playful chords.
In this cold, we find the fun,
Summer's sun? We just outrun!

Whispers of a Shimmering Tomorrow

Snowy whispers, secrets told,
Sleds like rockets, rough yet bold.
A cat in mittens prances around,
With every leap, a goofy sound.

The frost-covered trees wear crowns of ice,
Playful squirrels, oh what a slice!
They scamper about with fervent glee,
As if winter's a grand jubilee.

Snowball fights, our battles waged,
In icy fortresses, we're engaged.
But who knew icicles held such power?
A well-aimed toss, a cold shower!

Meet the snowflakes, each a prank,
With gleaming smiles, like tipsy clanks.
Tomorrow brings more snowy cheers,
As we giggle through the frosty years.

Celestial Radiance in a Chilled Embrace

Under the stars, the party glows,
With frosty cakes and squeaky shoes.
The bear in shades takes the stage,
As snowflakes dance, they're all the rage.

Comets crash—no, that's just snow,
But tumbling kids put on a show.
They roll and tumble, laughter rings,
Breaking the ice, like kings and queens.

The night is young, the frigid air,
A penguin slides without a care.
He flips and flops, what's that old joke?
Winter's fun is all bespoke.

Cosmic giggles blanket the ground,
In this frosty realm, joy is found.
While snowflakes twinkle, we all shout,
"Who needs the sun? Let's laugh it out!"

Beneath the Glittering Snowfall

Beneath the flakes, a secret plot,
Ice cubes rattle in a melting pot.
Sneaking hot fudge for a sweet delight,
While snowmen gossip through the night.

With fluffy hats and noses red,
We wear the snow like a crazy spread.
Measuring joy with every slack,
The hiccups follow as we laugh back.

Snow forts rise like ancient times,
Crafted with giggles, spiced with rhymes.
Yet every snowball flung with might,
Ends with a splash! Oh, what a sight!

So let us dance in this chilly bliss,
While mischief rules, how could we miss?
In winter's cradle, laughter will soar,
These gilded moments, who could ask for more?

Daisy Chains in Winter's Grasp

Snowflakes dance on icy ground,
Frosty friends come all around.
Wearing mittens, socks, and hats,
We build a snowman, where it's at!

Laughter echoes, snowballs fly,
A slippery slope, oh my, oh my!
With noses red and cheeks so bright,
We cherish this chilly delight.

Dreaming of blooms while we freeze,
We fashion chains with the greatest ease.
Lemonade will have to wait,
For now, it's fun within the fate!

So here we go with snowball fights,
And hot cocoa on winter nights.
With daisy chains made of snow,
We paint this season, don't you know?

Hidden Colors Beneath Snowblankets

Beneath the white, the colors hide,
A rainbow lost in winter's pride.
When snow melts down, they splash and glow,
Cerulean skies with a sunlit show.

Sledding down with swirls of glee,
Hidden shades we can't yet see.
We build a fort, a kingdom bright,
In hopes of colors taking flight.

Snowmen wearing hats so bright,
Look like clowns in the pale moonlight.
Under layers, we simply grin,
For warmth and laughter dwell within.

A secret world, so cold yet bold,
Where every story must be told.
Grab your sleigh and join the chase,
As we explore this frosty place!

Frigid Fantasies in Dusky Hues

Dreams of summer, frolic and play,
In winter's chill, we'll find a way.
With frosty beards and cheeks of pink,
We laugh aloud, not stop to think.

Penguins waddling, fashion on ice,
Making silly moves so nice.
Each snowflake wears a quirky hat,
Dancing round, imagine that!

In ice castles, we sip hot stew,
While snowmen sing with hey-hoo-hoo!
They twirl 'round with carrot nose flair,
As if the world has little care.

So grab your skates, let's take a whirl,
As laughter swirls in a chilly twirl.
With fantasies made of winter's muse,
We giggle under dusky hues!

The Magic of the Quieted Night

Stars are twinkling, oh what a sight,
In the silence of a snowy night.
Each flake whispers a story true,
Of snowmen tossing their hats askew.

Breath billows in puffs, so white,
As we frolic with all our might.
Who needs sleep when fun awaits?
In winter's arms, joy innervates.

Snow angels lie in peaceful repose,
With giggles blending with the snows.
Under the moon, we play our game,
The quiet night won't be the same.

With whispers soft and laughter grand,
We make our mark upon the land.
Amidst the quiet, we breathe in light,
And dance away in the chilly night!

Veils of White in a Silent World

Snowflakes tickle my nose,
My scarf's a tangled chaos.
Icicles hang, a shivering crew,
I slip on ice, what a brilliant show!

Puffs of breath become small clouds,
Squirrels giggle, gathering their crowds.
Snowmen wear hats that are far too wide,
With carrot noses, they seem to glide.

Laughter echoes in the chilly air,
I call for help, but none seem to care.
The ground's a slide in a winter wonk,
Turning the park into a funny prank!

An old dog, with fur like white fluff,
Dances in circles, barking enough.
Joy hides within the chilly breeze,
In this silent world, I find pure glee!

The Quiet of Winter's Breath

The trees wear coats of frosty lace,
As I waddle, my feet in a race.
With mittens stuffed and cheeks aglow,
I find my balance—oh no, not so!

A snowball's thrown and lands on me,
The dog's laughing; how can this be?
Chasing shadows, we aim and throw,
Yet somehow end up buried in snow!

Whispers of cold tickle my ears,
As penguins in hats soon draw near.
"Waddle like me!" they seem to decree,
While I slip and slide with glee!

Breezes carry giggles, oh what a sound,
In this quiet, joy is abound.
With snowy fluff and laughter so bright,
We dance in the shimmer of soft moonlight!

Melodies of a Frostbitten Night

Stars twinkle like bubbles in the sky,
While I juggle mittens and sigh.
The chill wraps around like an old friend,
But my feet refuse to bend!

A choir of owls hoot in delight,
As I trip on a branch, what a sight!
Fields of white dance beneath the moon,
I sing off-key to my own little tune.

Snowmen gossip, with noses so orange,
While I step back, my foot feels foreign.
Caught in a swirl, a snowy waltz,
A trip, a tumble, but who's at fault?

Frosty air brings cheer to my heart,
As nature's symphony plays its part.
With a wink and a laugh, I spin with glee,
Winter nights are a sparking jubilee!

Dreams Entwined in Crystal Webs

Spinning like a top in a flurry of white,
I chase my dreams on a snowy night.
Underneath the moon's frosty beam,
I tumble through ice, a whimsical dream!

Snowflakes swirl, casting spells so bright,
While I trip again — oh, what a fright!
A snowman offers me his carrot nose,
With a wink, he whispers, "Here's how it goes!"

Paths of glitter sparkle, I race and spin,
With puddles of frost, I jump right in.
Laughter erupts from every tree,
As the chill dances around me so free!

In this winter wonder, laughter's the thread,
Twirling and shouting, my worries are shed.
So here's to the fun in the snowy tale,
With joy in each flake, like an airborne sail!

Frosty Serenade of the Evening Sky

Stars in puffy coats prance about,
Snowflakes giggle, no room for doubt.
A snowman's hat, too big, it slips,
While winter's choir sings frosty quips.

Bunnies in boots make a crazy dash,
Slipping and sliding, oh, what a splash!
They laugh and tumble, no time to fret,
In a flurry of joy, they're not done yet.

Icicles hanging like shiny charms,
While gingerbread men plot their alarms.
With swirls and twirls, they dance and tease,
In a world of sparkle and icy breeze.

Beneath a moon that's grinning wide,
Chasing shadows, they cannot hide.
Under the laughter of this chilly sight,
The evening sky dances, oh what a delight!

The Allure of the White Horizon

Hats made of fluff and scarves galore,
Sleds zoom past with a hearty roar.
Snowballs fly, aimed with great care,
But somehow, they end in a kitty's hair!

Penguins in winter coats strut and sway,
Waddling around in their own ballet.
They trip on their toes, all in good fun,
Sliding on ice until they're done!

Toast by the fire with a cup so warm,
While marshmallows dance, oh what a charm!
Yet one went rogue, just like a star,
And splatted on the dog, oh, bizarre!

Snowmen are plotting a grand parade,
With carrot noses and hats they've made.
But just watch them fall, like they've lost the game,
Rolling around, oh, what a shame!

Timeless Tales in a Shimmering Frost

Whispers of winter weave their song,
In stories where giggles and snowflakes throng.
Frosty critters tell jokes so bright,
As they twinkle and shimmer in the soft moonlight.

A fox in a scarf, with a grin of glee,
Dances around like he's sipping tea.
With flurries of fun and a cheeky glance,
In a world of wonder, they all prance!

Squirrels in hats, with acorns to trade,
Creating a league, oh, such a charade.
They chatter and scatter, planning a feast,
For snowmen and bunnies, a jolly beast!

With every slope, a tale ignites,
Under the giggles of starry nights.
In this frosty land, no shadows of gloom,
Only laughter in the glittering room!

Dreams Traced in Winter's Embrace

Snowflakes drift like playful sprites,
Bringing giggles and snowy delights.
Underfoot they crunch and crack,
A winter dance on a joyful track.

Kittens in mittens, clumsy yet grand,
Rolling in snow, isn't it just planned?
With eyes full of mischief, they leap and bound,
Creating chaos, then flop with a sound.

At the corner, a kiddo slips on his skates,
With an elegant twist, he meets snow's fates.
Yet up he springs with a laugh so loud,
Sharing the fun, warming a crowd.

So here's to the wonder of wintertime woes,
In this magical world where each moment glows.
Where laughter and joy are as bright as the day,
In the sparkle of frost, all worries decay!

Starry Veil of Icebound Night

Tiny snowflakes dance with glee,
As I slip and slide like a clumsy bee.
The moon is laughing, what a sight,
As I start a snowball fight with a tree.

Chasing shadows, quite a chase,
With frosty breath, I make my case.
A snowman waves, I swear it's true,
But it's just my friend, in a frozen suit too.

The stars above wink in delight,
While I tumble down, oh what a fright!
I yell, "Look ma, no hands!" with flair,
But it's the snow that definitely wins this round of air.

Finally, I rest in the cold embrace,
My cheeks aglow, a rosy place.
With dreams of hot cocoa in my mind,
I snicker at the snow's sweet, icy grace.

Crystal Chimes in the Winter Air

Icicles hang like shimmering swords,
While penguins waddle, oh how absurd!
Snowflakes whisper the silliest tunes,
As I trip on my boots like a bunch of loons.

The wind blows soft, with a cheeky grin,
Telling secrets of where I've been.
I fashion a snowdog that gives me a bark,
But it's just a lump, oh that's just my mark.

Santa's sleigh got stuck in a tree,
Reindeer laughing; they're at a jubilee.
I take a sip of hot tea too hot,
And dance around, in my icy spot.

Chiming bells sound from a distant place,
While I smear snow on my friend's face.
With giggles echoing through the air,
How can winter be anything but fair?

Flickers of Light in a Frosted Fugue

Twinkling lights hang high and low,
As I pratfall in the drifts below.
A snowman nods, quite a cheeky fellow,
With a carrot nose, looking rather yellow.

Hot chocolate spills, what a sight,
I laugh, it's just my cocoa fight!
The frostbite tickles my nose in a dance,
As I strike a pose, but lose my pants!

Glittering frost on my friend's fluffy hat,
I tap-dance around, using my cat.
"Who needs a stage when there's snow to tread?"
As I plop in the fluff, feeling quite well-fed.

A snowball's whizzing, a close miss,
"Three points!" I shout, aiming for bliss.
We giggle until the sun dips low,
In this icy wonder, we steal the show.

Slightly Offbeat Melodies of Ice

Wobbly on skates, a sight to behold,
I twirl and I hop, my audacity bold.
The ice sings a tune, quite out of key,
As I try to impress a snow-loving bee.

Laughter erupts like a frosty spray,
With a snowball summoning my friend to play.
We build a fortress, our magical dome,
But end up just making cold ice-cream foam.

A penguin hero that struts to the beat,
With a belly flop dive, quite the feat!
The winter sun sets, and we spin around,
In this chilly kingdom, joy is found.

Naps taken in snow, a slightly warm space,
While the world spins round in a frosty embrace.
With every tumble, I find my own rhyme,
As we giggle and frolic, lost track of time.

Glimmering Frost Under the Moon

The moon's a giant disco ball,
Dancing on a frozen hall.
The snowmen busting out their moves,
While penguins give their groovy grooves.

A snowflake lands upon my nose,
And suddenly, I strike a pose.
The chilly air, a wild surprise,
As icicles form disco pies!

Hot cocoa brews with extra fluff,
But oh! It's way too hot and tough.
With marshmallows flying through the air,
It's a winter party everywhere!

When snowballs turn to playful fights,
The laughter echoes through the nights.
With frosty giggles, we all cheer,
In this chilly world, there's no fear!

Shards of Crystal Light

The sun throws sparkles on the street,
Like it's playing hide-and-seek!
With shades of blue and bright silver,
Each tiny flake begins to quiver.

Snowflakes whisper all around,
As ice skates screech upon the ground.
Twirling twirls with a whoosh and a whirl,
A frosty dancer starts to twirl.

But oh! A slip, and down I go,
My graceful moves become a show!
The ducks are laughing lakeside near,
At my winter ballet, oh dear!

With crystal lights from skies above,
The twinkling stars send frosty love.
We'll laugh and dance, no care in sight,
In this chilly wonder, pure delight!

Echoes of the Silent Snow

In silence falls the fluffy white,
A blanket soft, such pure delight.
But oh! What's that? A snowball flies,
The quiet turns to shouts and cries!

The snowman stands, a hat askew,
With a carrot nose that's lost its view.
He sneezes loud, and off it goes,
The laughter bursts; oh, how it grows!

The trees wear coats of glistening ice,
A slippery slide, oh, isn't it nice?
But watch your step, don't lose your way,
You might just slip and go astray!

With winter tunes sung in the night,
The echoes dance with pure delight.
We'll prance around with silly cheer,
In this frozen land, let's coerce a deer!

Chills in the Twilight

As twilight falls, it's time to chill,
A snowball count is quite the thrill.
Do folks in sleighs have secret spies?
Or is it just that sledding flies?

The frosty winds, they tickle toes,
And icicles hang like bright glow bows.
A squirrel darts, with mischief planned,
Look out below! Oh, snowy land!

The evening wraps us in its fold,
With stories of winter, tales retold.
Hot food waits on the kitchen's side,
While laughs and giggles swing and glide!

So let us raise our mugs with cheer,
To chilly fun, we hold so dear.
With frosty friends and snowy beams,
Let's celebrate these silly dreams!

Chasing Shadows in the Glittering Snow

A snowman wore a hat so tall,
He slipped and gave us all a fall.
The dogs all laughed as they raced by,
While squirrels waved, oh my, oh my!

Footprints dance in a zig-zag line,
Where penguin waddles seem divine.
Giggling friends, a snowball flight,
Oh what fun on this chilly night!

The snowflakes tumble in a swirl,
As I chase after a dizzy girl.
Her scarf unwinds, a bright red trail,
Together we create a grand snow tale!

In this world of white and bright,
We laugh until the morning light.
With frosty toes and cheeks aglow,
Our joy is sweet in winter's show!

Hazy Glimmers of a Silver Day

Once I found a glimmering spoon,
Left by a fairy in the afternoon.
Thought it was gold, oh what a sight,
Turned out to be just frozen light!

Hot cocoa spills, oh what a scene,
We built a fortress fit for a queen.
But as we laughed, it tumbled down,
Now we're just a snowy frown!

The sunlight twinkles, mischievous rays,
As shadows dance in silly ways.
We make a joke, a snowman cheer,
Where laughter lingers, winter dear!

With every carol sung out loud,
Our voices join the frosty crowd.
So here we stand, without dismay,
In a blissful, sparkly, silver day!

The Language of Snow and Starry Nights

On clear nights, the snowflakes giggle,
As I try to catch them and wiggle.
Each little flake has tales to tell,
From snowy hills to a frosty well!

Stars wink as they hear us shout,
"Let's make a snow angel out and about!"
Frosty halos, we laugh and tease,
While mice admire with bits of cheese!

The moon throws a party, what a blast,
With shadows that jump and dance so fast.
It's a waltz of mischief in the night,
Where every snowball is pure delight!

So let's embrace the winter cheer,
With a smile, a snowball, and nothing to fear.
In the cool, crisp night, we sing our song,
A harmony where we all belong!

Treading Softly on Whispering White

In the morning, the world's a cake,
With icing sugar, for goodness' sake!
I tiptoe lightly, not making a sound,
Until I slip, then tumble around!

The trees wear coats of powdery fluff,
While children gather, they've had enough.
Snowball fights and cheers fill the air,
Laughter bouncing everywhere!

The snow softly whispers, a secret song,
As friendly snowmen sing along.
Each footstep crunches, a silly beat,
While winter mischief dances on our feet!

We spin and twirl in a winter rave,
Until we land on the crispy pave.
With giggles and joy, we stay so bright,
Treading softly in the frosty light!

Twilight's Glare on a Crystal Path

Outside the door, snowflakes dance,
Like little elves in a clumsy prance.
I tripped on ice, oh what a sight,
My face in snow, a true delight.

The moonlit sparkles tease and play,
As raccoons join in the midday fray.
They knock the trash, a wild parade,
Dreams of warm soup begin to fade.

With frosty breath, I shout with glee,
This winter chill just isn't for me.
But hot cocoa awaits, oh what a treat,
With marshmallows plopped, it's hard to beat.

So slip and slide, give that a whirl,
In the winter's chill, let laughter twirl.
We'll make snowmen with silly hats,
Then race the dogs, and everyone laughs.

Ethereal Frost: Shards of Memory

In the morning light, the world freeze-framed,\nIcicles hang like pearls, all unclaimed.
My mittens vanish, seemed like a joke,
Turns out the dog thought they were his cloak.

Snowballs fly with a whoosh and a plop,
While Grandma's weathervane goes "bloop" and "lop."
We slip on the slope, trying hard not to fall,
A snowman's hat becomes a game after all.

At the park, sledding down a hill,
The wind in my hair, quite the thrill.
As I zoom by, I yell, "Woohoo!"
While my friend shrieked, "I'm stuck like glue!"

So gather 'round, let's share our cheer,
With funny fumbles that bring us near.
Hot pies cooling on the windowsill,
A winter's day, full of laughter still.

The Glistening Pathways of Chill

With every step, I slip and slide,
Laughing at my skills, or lack of pride.
My boots are slick, they do a jig,
It's winter's time for a funny gig.

Out in the snow, I squeak and squawk,
Talking to squirrels, having a talk.
They stop to stare and flick their tails,
As if to say, "You've missed the trails!"

Chasing flurries that dance and swirl,
Catch one quick, but it's quite a whirl.
Now lost my hat, oh, where did it go?
The wind laughs loudly and steals the show.

As dusk settles, the stars come bright,
And laughter echoes through the chilly night.
A snowball fight under the moon's soft beam,
Forget my first fall, I'm living the dream.

Whispers of Icy Night

The stars above wink and twinkle bright,
While snow owls hoot in the frosty night.
Slipping on ice, I make quite a sound,
Shouting at shadows that dance all around.

A snowflake falls right on my nose,
It makes me giggle; that everybody knows.
How could something so small, with grace like a queen,
Make me feel like a winter scene?

The laughter of friends fills the frozen air,
As snowmen come to life, with a bit of flair.
We give them scarves, and hats that don't fit,
Crafty creations; winter's bit jest.

So let the world freeze, it's all in good fun,
With warmth in our hearts, and cheeks red as sun.
Through the whispers of night, we find our way,
With joy that glimmers and music that plays.

Enchanted Dreams on a Glacial Canvas

In the park, penguins dance with flair,
A snowman winks, unaware of his hair.
With mittens on, we skip and slide,
Chasing snowflakes, wide-eyed with pride.

Hot cocoa spills, a marshmallow float,
Giggling at squirrels in their winter coat.
Ice skates twirl like a playful dream,
While snowballs blast and launch a scream.

A snow angel flops, but doesn't quite land,
Fluffy tops of snow, Michael's new band.
Frosty hats tipped as our noses all pink,
Winter's a laugh, more fun than you think!

So, let's build a palace, a couple of rooms,
With pickle-shaped towers and jellybean blooms.
In blizzard we dance, let the fun never cease,
Tomorrow's forecast? Chilly joy and peace!

Echoes of Light in the Winter Still

The sun peeks out in a giggling glow,
Twinkling lights shimmer on ice below.
Snowflakes flap like wings in the air,
Tickling noses, a frosty affair!

Laughter erupts, as we slip on the ice,
Ninj-skiing stunts that come without a price.
A cat in a scarf watches us fall,
While we brush off snow to have a snowball!

Hot cider spurts, burn my lip, oh dear!
Off comes my hat, let the winter cheer.
We play peek-a-boo with a tree made of glee,
Finding lost mittens and a squirrel's decree!

As daylight dims, the hoot owls jab,
And we share each tumble, a winter fab.
Cuddled in quilts, we gawk at the night,
The laughter remains, in this frosty delight!

Spheres of Frost in a Dreamscape

In the yard, round balls of snow collide,
With laughter echoing far and wide.
A snooze on a sled makes a cozy bed,
All while a raccoon raids the bread!

Silly hats atop our heads so tall,
And carrots for noses, we've got them all!
A snowball fight flings giggles so bright,
As we dance around like fireflies at night.

Frostbite tugs while we're crafting a scene,
A slushy masterpiece of cottony sheen.
Fingers are numb, but the smiles never fade,
Jumpy bundling, a winter parade!

In moonlight, we find a wobbly trail,
Following giggles like a tall tale.
Tired but giddy, we head back to jest,
Wrapped in warm laughter, we're truly blessed.

Luminescent Shadows of the Chill

Bouncing around like a rubbery snow,
Shadows flicker, light twinkles, oh no!
Snowmen frolic while wearing a grin,
Their carrot-nosed secrets, joking within.

Snowball machines powered by giggly glee,
A quick missle dodge, adorned in cotton candy!
Flapping flags made of paper and sticks,
Lite Up Night makes our hearts do tricks.

Cocoa stands tall like a wintery king,
Where marshmallow swans make the bellies sing.
The mistletoe hangs, but we just throw balls,
As shadows pirouette and tap on the walls.

Sledges and laughter, a magical ride,
Playing this game with many a slide.
Bringing the giggles 'til the sun takes its claim,
To shimmer in shadows, we'll always be game!

Enchanted Snowfall and Winter Whispers

Snowflakes dance like sugar sprites,
Chasing tails on frosty nights.
I slip and slide, what a show,
Oh, where's my grace? I do not know!

Children laugh, a snowball fight,
Dodge my target, oh what fright!
A mitten lost, my nose a rose,
Winter's antics, none oppose!

Frosty breath, my scarf's a mess,
I wear it proud, I must confess.
Laughter erupts, as I take a dive,
In this blanket, I feel alive!

So let it snow, on frosty ground,
With silly jumps, joy's always found.
Each frosty breath, a giggle shared,
Winter's charm, none can be spared!

Winter's Grace in the Dimmed Light

Icicles hang like swords of ice,
A chin-up man said it was nice.
But when I slipped and caught my breath,
I think this cold might lead to death!

Snowmen wave with carrot grins,
While I faceplant, oh the sins!
My dignity lost, but who's to care?
In this winter wonder, fun's the flair!

Hot cocoa spills while I exclaim,
This chilly game is truly lame!
Yet as I laugh with friends so dear,
I cherish winter, year by year!

So here's a toast to frosty cheer,
With snowy socks and hearts sincere.
A waltz with flakes, let's give a cheer,
For giggles reign when winter's here!

Beneath the Snow, Heartbeats of Dreams

Under blankets, snug and tight,
A pillow fort, oh what a sight!
Outside snowflakes weave their thread,
While I nap, dreams dance in my head.

Snow boots squeak, a quirky sound,
But how I wish to twirl around!
A wicked slip, and down I go,
My friends all laugh, love this show!

Hot soup steams in my favorite mug,
Yet someone's brought a rubber bug!
With all the squeals that break the calm,
Winter mischief, what a charm!

So hoot and holler, embrace the chill,
Winter's antics bring such thrill.
Heartbeats pulse beneath the snow,
In laughter's warmth, our spirits grow!

Starlight Echoes on Frozen Water

Stars above in a frosty sky,
I slip and flop, oh me, oh my!
On frozen lakes, we glide and spin,
But wait! What's this? My pants are thin!

Ice skates clack, a waltz of sorts,
Ballet falls turned into sports!
With every tumble, giggles swell,
I'm the star of the icy spell!

A mischievous pup joins in the spree,
With joyful barks, he's wild and free.
We chase the moonlight, fast and bright,
Laughter echoes through the night!

So let the stars inspire delight,
In every slip and twinkling light.
Dance through winter's chilly sway,
In laughter's glow, we'll pounce and play!

Crystal Echoes of Silent Hues

In a land where snowmen wear hats,
And penguins dance on chilly mats,
Icicles hang like glittery swords,
While squirrels plot their winter hoards.

Snowflakes tumble, not always right,
They land on noses, what a sight!
Hot cocoa spills from mugs of cheer,
As marshmallows hide, oh dear, oh dear!

Frosty whispers in the bright sun,
'Tis not the wind, it's winter fun!
With goofy grins on everyone,
We laugh and trip; oh, what a run!

Beneath the glow of moonlit shows,
Surprises hide in frosty toes.
In the chill, we all unite,
In funny hats, we dance the night!

The Quiet Dance of Winter's Breath

Snowflakes twirl on a silent stage,
Little critters dance, set free, uncaged.
The cold is crisp, the air is tight,
Yet mischief blooms beneath the light.

Polar bears slip on icy acts,
While bunny hops create some facts.
In winter's glow, they have their say,
Making snow angels lead the way!

Shivers sent from a lost sock,
Turns into laughter—what a shock!
Snowball fights in a chilly spree,
Winter's breath, let it be a glee!

As starlit skies drape the cold,
Our winter tales are joyfully told.
With giggles bright on the frosty trails,
We dance and spin, as laughter prevails!

Tinsel Threads in the Cold

Tinsel shimmer and lights aglow,
While reindeer prance in the frosty show.
The snowman grins, a carrot nose,
In winter tales, silliness grows.

Mitten mishaps and funny slips,
Sleds that fly with laugh-filled trips.
Icicles sparkle, a show of spark,
As friends collide—we laugh 'til dark!

Carols echo through the trees,
Notes are flat, yet bring us ease.
Dance around the evergreen,
In silly socks, we reign supreme!

Hot drinks spill and giggles burst,
In this cold, we quench our thirst.
Through the frosty, dizzy spins,
Laughter's where the fun begins!

Ethereal Slumber on Silver Sheets

As blankets fall of snowy white,
Naps in the sun bring pure delight.
Frosty pillows and dreams that gleam,
We snooze like bears, in cozy cream.

Winter whispers secrets low,
Of silly snores that steal the show.
Fluffy flakes on sleepyhead,
Waking up is not in the thread!

In fluffy pajamas, dreams run wild,
With snowflakes teasing every child.
Winter's blanket makes us beam,
As we awake from our sweet dream!

Laughter echoes through the chill,
Hot cocoa's warmth, it's quite a thrill.
In this slumber, joy unfolds,
With each new day, the fun retold!

Lullabies of a Frigid Dawn

In the chill of dawn, a penguin did sing,
Woke up the snowflakes, gave each a fling.
They laughed and they twirled, what a sight to see,
As the frost on the window turned to a spree.

A squirrel in mittens, quite proud of its flair,
Danced on the ice, without a single care.
He slipped and he slid, oh, what a ballet,
While the frosty trees giggled, oh what a play!

A snowman with style, sporting a hat,
Winks at the sun—imagine that!
He tells all the birds, "Do dance on my head,"
While they squawk and they peck, they're easily fed.

As the skies cast their glow, the day takes its turn,
The chill brings delight, and hearts brightly burn.
In a world dressed in white, let laughter unfold,
For amid all the frost, sweet stories are told.

Glistening Mirage of the Unseen

A snowflake fell softly on a cat's little nose,
The feline sneezed loudly, which startled a rose.
It giggled and danced, saying, "Oh, what a prank!"
While the moon shook its head at the hillside flank.

A rabbit in glasses, reading a tome,
Proclaimed snowball fights far better than home.
He hopped through the drifts, a sight quite absurd,
Challenging snowflakes, "You're all quite unheard!"

The sun made a face, then slipped on a suit,
To join in the playtime, making everyone hoot.
A warm laugh echoed through the glimmering glade,
As snowmen exchanged their warm mittens, displayed.

With all of this play, who could whine or mope?
Each shimmer and sparkle brought little hearts hope.
In this mirthful ballet, where the frosty winds breeze,
Life's silly enchantments put minds at such ease.

The Stillness of Enchanted Frost

In the still of the night, a bear walked in style,
Wore a tutu of snow, oh, it's been a while!
He pranced through the whiteness, a sight to behold,
While trees whispered softly, their stories retold.

A fox with a scarf, tinged bright as a dream,
Told the owls to hoot, "Let's form our cool team!"
With a wink and a grin, they devised quite a plot,
For a snowball parade, like it or not!

The chill in the air, carried giggles, quite fleet,
As a deer tap-danced on the crystalline street.
With joy in her heart, she spun like a dart,
Turning winter's hush into a masterpiece art.

As night drifts along, and stars light the way,
The world feels alive, and everyone plays.
For in chilly embraces, with laughter we toast,
In stillness, we find, it's the fun we love most.

Hypnotic Patterns in Snowdrift

A snowflake arriving, with flair and a dream,
Found friends in a snowdrift, plotting a scheme.
They whirled and they twirled, like dancers on ice,
As the weather, bemused, thought it's all quite nice.

A penguin in shades caught the frosty sun's rays,
Declared it a day for his beachy displays.
He slid down the hill, with no hint of fear,
Claiming, "Watch out, my friends, the carnival's here!"

Frosty sparkles murmured, "What's this fun dance?"
While snowmen conspired to join in the chance.
With carrot noses jiving to unknown beats,
The rhythm held tight 'round chilly retreats.

In this whimsical chill, where laughter takes flight,
Everything's funny in this frosty delight.
So raise up your mittens, let's cheer 'til we glow,
For in quilts made of snow, pure joy's in the flow!

Ethereal Glaze and Frozen Wishes

A snowman lost his hat, oh dear!
Frosty winds whisper, come here!
He's wearing carrots for a nose,
But where's his scarf? I suppose he froze.

Chilly gnomes dance with great delight,
Slipping and sliding under moonlight.
Icicles drip like silly jokes,
While polar bears don their winter cloaks.

Penguins waddle, quite the parade,
Ice skates squeak, but they're not afraid.
Snowflakes giggle as they float down,
Colorful laughter in the white town.

Frolicking children build a fort,
Snowball fights of the grandest sort!
As winter whispers jokes in the night,
Mirthful spirits take to flight.

Beneath the Chill, a Whisper of Warmth

Underneath blankets, we snuggle tight,
Hot cocoa bubbles, what a sight!
Marshmallows float like snow in a cup,
Sipping with glee, oh fill me up!

Frogs in hats dance a winter jig,
While snowflakes fall, the night feels big.
Chasing chimeras of snowman plots,
Winter's humor is what we've got.

The cat wears boots, snug and round,
Sliding across this frosty ground.
Sledding down hills, a whoosh and a spin!
Cheerful blunders, let the fun begin!

As the cold wraps the world in white,
Warmth in our hearts keeps us bright.
Every giggle echoes like chimes,
In this crazy dance of winter rhymes.

A Tapestry of Frosted Dreams

Knitted mittens hang from a tree,
Why did they leave their owner, me?
They giggle softly, 'Oh what a shame!'
Socks join in, playing the same game.

Snowflakes prance, so sprightly and bold,
They tickle noses, never too cold.
Slippery sidewalks, a circus show,
Mama's advice: 'Take it slow!'

The dog's in trouble, stuck on a hill,
Chasing squirrels with a heart to thrill.
Blizzards howl, it's a howling fun,
While everyone dreams of the next big run!

Count your blessings, as snowflakes fall,
Joyful giggles, let's share them all.
With laughter echoing through the night,
We create magic, oh what a sight!

Starlit Chill and Glacial Touch

Under stars, the chill takes flight,
While snowmen gossip all through the night.
Bouncing rabbits in coats of white,
Sipping on snowflakes, feels quite right.

Twinkling lights on a frosty wall,
Christmas cookies, let's have a ball!
Sugar rushes speed through our veins,
Crash course in winter, but who complains?

With snowball targets and sledding cheers,
Our breath makes clouds, brightening fears.
Each little slip and fall brings glee,
As laughter rings through our frosty spree.

So here we are, in the winter's glee,
Chasing chill and warm memories.
With every giggle under the moon,
We find joy in winter's playful tune.

Glacial Reveries

The snowman wears a silly hat,
His carrot nose is quite a brat.
With dancing snowflakes in the air,
He often trips without a care.

Sledding down the hill so fast,
I scream a shout; I'm quite the blast.
But when I land, I flop like meat,
And giggle as I ice my feet.

A penguin slide, an arctic race,
I try to join, but have no grace.
They waddle by with gleeful glee,
While I just laugh beneath a tree.

With snowball fights and frosty cheer,
The winter breeze is full of cheer.
So let us play before it melts,
And count the joy within our belts.

Hushed Wishes on Snowdrifts

In the quiet, snowflakes fall,
Whispering secrets, oh so small.
A snowcat pounces, unaware,
And lands on me—I flip in air!

A snow angel flaps and spreads her wings,
While rubber boots hop, and laughter rings.
The frosty bite makes noses red,
My cheeks pop back—who needs a bed?

Hot cocoa spills upon my shoe,
A marshmallow misfit, oh, what a view!
I sip and slide, the world's a joke,
As icicles dangle from each oak.

With every crunch and frosty sound,
I twirl and tumble on this ground.
The tales we weave, they dance and twine,
As winter's charm starts to entwine.

Reflections in a Glassy Pane

Through the window, I chance to see,
A snowflake lands right on my tea.
It twirls and dives, a little sprite,
And makes my drink a snowy fright!

The kids outside do somersaults,
While I am stuck with tea that halts.
I cheer for them, all bouncy and bright,
While sipping slowly 'til its night.

The glass reflects my silly grin,
As outside, snowmen wear a tin.
I join them soon for a frosty chat,
And trade some joy with a dancing cat.

The evening glows with stars on high,
As winter's whimsy passes by.
With cozy dreams upon my mind,
I'll dance with laughter, oh so blind.

Silver Shadows Beneath the Stars

In a blanket wrapped, I start to stare,
At dancing skies, quite strange and rare.
My friends all join with jokes and cheer,
While shadows creep; we've naught to fear.

The moonlight glints upon our toes,
We try to walk, but tumble, oh no!
Giggles echo through the night,
As snowballs fly, oh, what a sight!

With silver beams on icy trails,
We create tales of snowy gales.
Each frosty moment brings delight,
As laughter twirls in winter's bite.

So here's to fun beneath the glow,
Where silver shadows gleefully flow.
We'll dance and joke 'til dawn arises,
In winter's charm, we've found our prizes.

Crystalline Whispers of What Was

In the chilly air, a snowman pranced,
His carrot nose seemed quite entranced.
He winked at the kids, gave a little jig,
Then slipped on ice, became quite big!

Frosty laughs echoed through the street,
As kittens chased tails, oh what a feat!
A snowball fight turned into a mess,
Who knew winter could cause such distress?

Icicles hang like chandeliers bright,
While penguins debate who'll take flight.
They ice skate on ponds with a whirly spin,
Chasing frosty bunnies, let the games begin!

So as the flakes begin to twirl,
Join in the giggles, give joy a whirl!
For laughter is found in every flake,
In this winter wonder, let's shake and bake!

Twilight's Embrace in the Arctic Air

Under twilight skies with stars that shine,
The polar bears dance, looking so fine.
They twirl in circles, quite out of sync,
While seals laugh hard, just on the brink.

Snowmen gossip about their ice cream hats,
While rabbits hop alongside the chitchats.
A penguin slips, gives a comical shout,
As we all burst into giggles, no doubt!

A sleigh took off with reindeer in tow,
But one lost a sock, oh what a show!
They zoom through the stars, laughter in tow,
In this winter evening, joy starts to flow.

So wrap up warm, and join the parade,
In the frosty air, let's not be dismayed!
For amidst the chill, warmth starts to bloom,
With funny moments that fill up the room.

Snowflakes Sing of Forgotten Journeys

As snowflakes tumble, they sing a tune,
Of rabbits skidding under the moon.
One missed its chance, landed in a stew,
While owls hooted, 'What's wrong with you?'

A tiny snowball flew right past my head,
I think it was thrown by a bird with dread.
He tried to fly home with a cheeky grin,
But tripped on ice, let the fun begin!

Children built forts and claimed their land,
With snowball cannons that make quite a stand.
But one little boy spent too long inside,
Emerging with snowballs as big as his pride!

Through frosty skies, the giggles rise,
In this winter realm, laughter never dies.
So catch a snowflake, give it a twirl,
In the chill of the night, let your laughter unfurl!

Quicksilver Visions of the Night

In quicksilver moments, the night takes flight,
With snowflakes twirling, oh what a sight!
A raccoon in boots dances near a wall,
He tumbles and tumbles, then makes a call!

Chilly winds whistle a merry song,
While mice in top hats break out in throng.
They skate on the pond with flair and style,
And leave us in stitches, laughter's the dial!

Under the moon, a penguin takes a dive,
Into a snowbank, where he'll surely thrive.
Meanwhile, the snowflakes giggle in glee,
As they plan a parade for all to see!

So gather your friends for a night full of cheer,
In the whimsical winter, let's give a cheer!
For in every flake, a chuckle is trapped,
Let's dance through the night, happily wrapped!

The Cold Embrace of Time

A snowman with a carrot nose,
Wonders why his feet are froze.
He tries to dance, slips on his side,
Laughing, he says, "What a frosty ride!"

Icicles hang like teeth of fate,
I swear they're jesting, oh how they wait.
A penguin slides by, winks at the sun,
"I'll race you!" he shouts, and oh, what fun!

The clock ticks slow in chilly air,
While squirrels in jackets plot their dare.
Chasing snowflakes with a goofy cheer,
Who knew winter could bring such gear?

Hot cocoa spills; marshmallows fly,
A snowball fight makes the neighbors sigh.
With snowflakes caught in giggles and shouts,
Winter feels warm with laughter about!

Silhouettes Against a Snowy Canvas

A cat in boots, keep your paws here!
Prowling in snow, with a chirpy sneer.
She leaps and bounds, slips on her tail,
Laughing at the frost, she tells a tale.

The trees wear blankets, oh what a sight,
Whispers of winds, a giggling flight.
Birds in scarves sing off-pitch tunes,
While snowflakes fall like silly balloons.

A waddling penguin on a toboggan,
His laugh echoes like a bright dragon.
With a splash into powdery fluff,
He claims, "That's it! I've had enough!"

Stars twinkle in all their clumsy grace,
Snowflakes giggle, not wanting to race.
In this winter, with gleams that please,
Life's a dance with the blustery breeze.

Enshadowed Dreams Beneath the Ice

Underneath the snow, do they snore?
Teddy bears in icebergs, what a score!
They planned a party in a frosty den,
But all they've got is ten frozen men.

Skates on rabbits, tumbling with glee,
Chasing their tails—oh, wacky spree!
They giggle and hop, their tails a blur,
Creating snow angels, a feathery stir.

Ghosts of winter, with their chilly breath,
Dance 'neath the stars, defying death.
They pull silly pranks, like ice cream fights,
While the sun rolls out, igniting the nights.

So here's to the shadows that tease the light,
For smiles come easy on frosty nights.
Though dreams may be wrapped in a cool embrace,
The laughter we share makes the world a place!

Night's Embrace and Light's Retreat

When night wraps all in a silver glow,
Bobby the owl shouts, "Who's ready to go?"
With sparkling stars as his party hat,
He swoops and dives, and—oh, where's the cat?

In a field of snow, with laughter strange,
Moose learns to tango, oh what a change!
His hooves get tangled in snowy threads,
"Wait! Was this dance on my calendar?" he dreads.

Snowflakes twirl and whisper a joke,
As the moon joins in with a shy poke.
"A dance off sounds splendid, come one, come all,"
But the frosty breeze makes everyone stall.

Yet laughter echoes in the chilly hush,
When penguins arrive in a joyous rush.
As night grows old, joy takes its seat,
In this blizzard of silliness, who can compete?

Chill of Midnight Whispers

When snowflakes dance like giggling sprites,
The moonlight tickles the frosty nights.
A penguin slips on ice with glee,
Wearing a hat, as cool as can be.

A snowman sneezes, 'Oh what a sight!'
His carrot nose takes flight in the night.
With frosty breath, he starts to hum,
A jolly tune, like a party drum.

Laughter echoes through the chilly air,
A polar bear in pajamas — what a flair!
Frosty giggles from trees up high,
Even the owls can't help but sigh.

So grab a hot cocoa, take a seat,
As winter's antics dance on your street.
In these nights where silliness reclaims,
Life's a laugh, despite the cold flames.

Glimmers in the Icebound Night

Stars are winking in icy cheer,
While squirrels play cards, oh dear, oh dear!
The snowman claims he's a world-class chef,
Serving up snowballs, with a side of jest.

A snowflake lands on a cat's warm paw,
It meows in shock, 'Is this winter's law?'
The rabbit hops with a giggling hop,
As hot cocoa spills, and he can't stop!

Frosty friends in a snowball fight,
Sideways roll, oh what a sight!
With snowflakes flying high and wide,
Every laughing face there is filled with pride.

Under the moon, the fun will last,
As winter's mischief is unsurpassed.
In icebound nights where spirits soar,
Hilarity reigns, forever more.

Shimmering Thoughts Beneath Snow

Beneath the blanket of sparkling white,
Bunnies are plotting their great delight.
One says, 'Let's build a fort today!'
While onlookers cheer, 'Hip hip hooray!'

Giddy snowflakes swirl, dance and twirl,
While a dog dreams of a snowball whirl.
'Tis the season for laughter, so abundant,
As ice sculptures giggle, oh how redundant!

A frosty breeze whispers a silly tune,
A prancing raccoon beneath the moon.
With snowmen laughing and cats gone wild,
Even the grumpiest of hearts feel riled.

With warm mugs in hand, friends come outside,
To share in the frolic, no need to hide.
For all the fun under white, soft fluff,
Makes winter's touch a little less tough.

Frosted Fantasies in Moonlight

In the hush of night, laughter twinkles bright,
With snowflakes laughing, causing delight.
A seal on a sled, what a curious sight,
Zooming down hills, full of sheer fright!

A snow globe spins, with a twist of fate,
Tiny trees jiggle and dance, feeling great.
The moon holds secrets of hearts lost in joy,
While a kid builds a rocket; it's made of old toys!

With marshmallow clouds floating so high,
Even winter's creatures let out a sigh.
Polar bears twirl in a comical show,
As frosty delights put on a very funny glow.

Under the stars, all worries drift away,
In frosted fantasies, we laugh and play.
So let's dive in, to the wonders of night,
For snowy dreams make the world so bright!

Milton Keynes UK
Ingram Content Group UK Ltd.
UKHW022342171124
451242UK00007B/107